ARMED FORCES
★ ★ ★

UNITED STATES
COAST GUARD

by Jack David

BELLWETHER MEDIA ★ MINNEAPOLIS, MN

Library of Congress
David, Jack, 1968–
  United States Coast Guard / by Jack David.
    p. cm. — (Torque: Armed Forces)
  Includes bibliographical references and index.
  ISBN-13: 978-1-60014-163-8 (hbk. : alk. paper)
  ISBN-10: 1-60014-163-3 (hbk. : alk. paper)
  1. United States. Coast Guard—Juvenile literature. I. Title.
  VG53.D38 2008
  363.28'60973—dc22   2007042408

CONTENTS

★ ★ ★

★ ★ ★

Chapter One

WHAT IS THE UNITED STATES COAST GUARD?

The Coast Guard's motto is *Semper Paratus*, which means "always ready" in Latin.

A United States Coast Guard ship speeds through rough water toward a sinking ship. The Coast Guard members will rescue the passengers and carry them to safety.

The Coast Guard is one branch of the **United States Armed Forces**. The other branches are the Air Force, Army, Marines Corps, and Navy. The five branches work together to protect the nation.

All branches of the U.S. Armed Forces are part of the U.S. government. The Coast Guard is considered part of the Department of Homeland Security. The other four branches are considered part of the Department of Defense.

The Coast Guard is a unique branch. It is the only one that does not fight battles. It still plays an important role in defending the United States. Coast Guard members use ships and boats to protect our shores. They stop people from entering the country illegally. They protect U.S. **ports** from attack. They track down **drug runners** and perform daring ocean rescues.

Chapter Two

VEHICLES, WEAPONS, AND TOOLS OF THE COAST GUARD

104

101

U. S.

U.

The Coast Guard started in 1790 as the United States Revenue Cutter Service.

Icebreakers

Ships are the most important Coast Guard vehicles. Coast Guard ships longer than 65 feet (19.8 meters) are called **cutters**. The largest cutters are **icebreakers**. They are built to plow through icy waters. Smaller cutters patrol coastlines and rivers.

Vessels under 65 feet (19.8 meters) in length are simply called boats. They usually stay close to shore. Port security boats keep ports safe. Motor life boats are built for sea rescues.

On an average day, the Coast Guard helps 114 people in trouble at sea.

The Coast Guard also uses aircraft. Planes such as the HC-130 Hercules can search a wide area for lost or missing ships. Helicopters such as the HH-65C Dolphin are used in water rescues. Rescuers can lower **harnesses** into the water. These are used to pull people out of the water and into the helicopter. The MH-68A Stingray is a helicopter armed with guns. Coast Guard members sometimes have to use guns to enforce laws.

MH-68A Stingray

Coast Guard members need lots of other equipment to do their jobs. Life vests and life rafts help people stay afloat during emergencies. Radios allow members to communicate with each other. Some Coast Guard members carry weapons. They may carry small pistols, rifles, or shotguns. They often use **nonlethal** ammunition to capture criminals.

Chapter Three

LIFE IN THE COAST GUARD

Basic training

very Coast Guard member has an important role. Each person has a **rank**. Most are **enlisted members.** These members start their service with eight weeks of **basic training** at the Coast Guard Training Center in New Jersey. They go through physical drills and classes. They learn about water survival, **seamanship**, and Coast Guard life. After this training, they get training for a specific job.

Officers

Officers are the leaders of the Coast Guard. They always hold ranks above those of enlisted members. Officers must have a college degree. They attend Officer Candidate School (OCS) at the United States Coast Guard Academy in Connecticut. There they learn advanced leadership and technical skills. By the end of this training, they are ready to lead other members of the Coast Guard.

Admiral is the highest rank a Coast Guard officer can earn.

GLOSSARY

★ ★ ★

basic training—the course of drills, tests, and military training that new enlisted members of every branch of the U.S. Armed Forces must go through

cutter—a Coast Guard ship; cutters measure longer than 65 feet (19.8 meters).

drug runners—people who transport illegal drugs

enlisted members—a person in the U.S. Armed Forces who ranks below an officer; all enlisted members are currently volunteers.

harness—a set of straps used to safely lift a person out of the water

icebreaker—a ship designed to break paths through ocean ice

nonlethal—not capable of causing death

officer—a member of a branch of the armed forces who ranks above enlisted members

port—a place where ships load and unload cargo

rank—a specific position and level of responsibility in a group

seamanship—the art of handling and navigating a ship at sea

United States Armed Forces—the five branches of the United States military; they are the Air Force, the Army, the Coast Guard, the Marines Corps, and the Navy.

TO LEARN MORE

★ ★ ★

AT THE LIBRARY

Braulick, Carrie A. *U.S. Coast Guard Cutters.* Mankato, Minn.: Capstone, 2007.

Cooper, Jason. *U.S. Coast Guard.* Vero Beach, Fla.: Rourke, 2004.

Randolph, Joanne. *Coast Guard Boats To The Rescue!* New York: Rosen, 2008.

ON THE WEB

Learning more about the United States Coast Guard is as easy as 1, 2, 3.

1. Go to www.factsurfer.com

2. Enter "Coast Guard" into search box.

3. Click the "Surf" button and you will see a list of related web sites.

With factsurfer.com, finding more information is just a click away.

INDEX

★ ★ ★

The images in this book are reproduced through the courtesy of the United States Department of Defense.